Table of Contents

D0109410

Jerry Baker
America's Master Gardener®

Introduction

Man has pursued the beauty of flowers for thousands of years, and today, flower gardening is more popular than ever before. So if you're planning on adding a flower garden, patio container, or hanging basket of flowers to your porch, patio, or along your walk and driveways, take some time to read this booklet before you begin. You'll learn a little something about each of the groups of flowers that are available, how to plant, feed and water them, and you may just save yourself time, money and effort in the process! And you won't have the grief, aggravation, and disappointment that most new flower growers face.

Now some of my tips, tricks, and tonics may seem strange to you, but in the end, it's the results that count. And you can't help but have fabulous flowers if you follow my simple steps to floral success!

If you have a flower or flower care question, why don't you call me **"On the Garden Line,"** Saturday mornings from 8:00 a.m. - 10:00 a.m. EST on your local Mutual Broadcasting Station. The toll-free number is **1-800-634-3881.**

Also, for more comprehensive information, please refer to one of my other full-size books:

Plants Are Still Like People
Jerry Baker's Flowering Garden
The Impatient Gardener

or pick up a copy of **America's Gardening Newsletter, "On The Garden Line®,"** which is also jam-packed with timely tips, tricks and tonics on lawn, garden and house plant care.

VARIETIES

Annuals, perennials, biennials, wild flowers, bulbs and bulb types are pretty much the menu available for the home gardener's taste. Let me tell you folks, there is enough of a selection on your local garden centers' shelves that it would take you dozens of years and hundreds of garden patches to digest and plant them all. So in this booklet, we are going to concentrate on the most popular varieties. But first, let me give you a thumb-nail sketch of each of the categories:

ANNUALS

Simply put, an annual is a plant that starts from an early spring or late winter planted seed, germinates, sprouts, grows to adulthood, flowers, and dies all in the same season. If the flower is left on the stem, it will set new seeds, develop, mature, fall off or be collected for replanting next season.

PERENNIALS

This group of plants is best described by saying that they live several years, enduring the changes of season without your help to return in blooming splendor year after year. There is, however, 1 catch: not all perennials can make it on their own in certain parts of the country without your help, but we will discuss that later. For the time being, let's say that perennials have an average life span of 3 to 5 years. This makes them "odds-on" favorites with most experienced gardeners.

🌼 VARIETIES

BIENNIALS

This flower group is the bridge between the short lived annuals and the longer producing perennials. Biennials are sown in late fall or early spring, sprout and grow through the summer, go dormant in fall, and bloom like the dickens the following spring, completing their life cycle in 2 years.

WILD FLOWERS

This describes a pattern of growth behavior as opposed to a type of plant. Wild flower collections are combinations of seeds from all 3 of the above groups.

BULBS

This plant group needs no special introduction to the seasoned gardener. The average home gardener, however, has not yet discovered the value of bulbs when it comes to both the beauty they can add and the gardener's pocketbook.

BULB TYPES

Professionally, we refer to these little gems as corms and tubers. What bulbs, corms, and tubers have in common is that they all store food for growing their foliage and flowers. Your should note that if you live in the below-freezing areas of the country, you must dig up and store many of the corms and tubers, and all of the summer flowering bulbs.

With that introduction out of the way, we can now get down to the serious business of planning and selection.

TOOLS

As I meander through the aisles of my local garden centers, I am disappointed in the spending habits of the average home gardener when it comes to garden tools. I frequently overhear, "Don't you have something cheaper?" Well, they most certainly do! Today's modern retailer didn't just fall off a turnip truck! They subscribe to the words from an old Broadway musical, "Find out what they want, and give it to them just that way."

If you want garden success, use the best quality tools you can buy. If you can't afford hardwood-handled, heavy steel-bladed tools today, then do without, and save until you can afford them. Here is a list of tools that you should acquire over time for all of your garden chores:

A flat-backed, square-bladed shovel; a long-handled, pointed shovel; a 4-pronged spading fork; a flat-backed garden rake; a metal leaf rake; a swae hoe; a trowel (medium width); a dibble; a blocking hoe; and a #10 bastard file.

TIMELY TOOL TIPS

• On all of your long-handled tools, mark off, by the inch, from the top to the bottom with a file. Then use stain or ink in the file mark so that you always have a measuring device handy.

• Always paint part of the lower handle and the top of the steel of your tools with a combination of color stripes to identify them as yours. That way, when they walk over to your neighbors' garage, you'll be able to identify them. It also makes them easier to find when you lay them down in the grass.

• Keep all of the blades and points sharp with the bastard file.

• Cover all sharp edges with small pieces of old garden hose that have been slit to fit over the blades or tips.

• Never put any of your tools away dirty. Wash and dry them, and then lightly spray with either WD-40 or Pam®.

Jerry Baker
America's / Master Gardener®

LOCATION

I've got three words that tell you everything you need to have the best flower garden in town: location, location, location. It never fails that wherever you need or want flowers to grow, it turns out to be in deep shade, under water, or in solid concrete. There is no getting around it, all flowers need good soil to grow in. Any soil, however, can be improved with the proper additives, or you can raise your beds above the problem, hang them over top of it, or set them in pots or on stands. The cardinal rule is that you must **make your flowers comfortable!**

There is a type of flower to fit almost any location that you can think of. The trick is taking the time to find it. I suggest that you keep a supply of the major mail order seed catalogs handy to guide you in your selection. These catalogues are a Godsend to both you and your flowers.

STARTING SEEDS
Indoors

Are you kidding? "You want me to wait for seeds to sprout, transplant them, worry that they'll wilt—not me. At my age, I don't even buy green bananas." That's the outburst from a gardener friend of mine when I suggested that he start his own plants from seed. He was dissatisfied with the seedlings he had bought last year, so he agreed to at least consider taking on this homegrown project.

Why should anyone consider starting seeds from scratch, when seedlings are available almost anywhere? Consider these pluses: when you start your own plants from seed, you know they're healthy, hardy, and disease-free You'll also save money because seeds cost a fraction of seedlings.

On the other hand, my friend's comments about the extra effort were right. You have to wait for seeds to sprout, and you need to transplant them. The benefits, however, far outweigh the inconveniences. So, for those of you who want to grow plants from scratch, here are some hints to help you along.

SELECT SEEDS WITH CARE:

Don't buy last year's seeds! Start with fresh harvest seed from a reputable firm; each package is stamped with the year for planting. Here are some reputable companies that will send you a free catalog upon request:

W. Atlee Burpee Co., 300 Park Ave., Warminister, PA 18974
Johnny's Selected Seeds, 310 Foss Hill Road, Albion, ME 04910
Park Seed Co., Box 46, Greenwood, SC 29648
Stokes Seeds, Inc., Box 548, Buffalo, NY 14240
Thompson & Morgan, Box 1308, Jackson, NJ 08527

When you're selecting seeds, look for "virus free" varieties. These seeds are guaranteed to be from plants that had no viruses. Purchase the smallest amount available for your needs. Assume that each seed will sprout, and unless you have 40 acres to spare, 1 ounce of tomato seeds is a bigger bite than you can chew.

America's / Master Gardener®

🏠 STARTING SEEDS INDOORS

The day your seeds arrive, put them in the refrigerator until you are ready to plant them indoors. But don't do this any sooner than 6 weeks before the last killing frost in your area.

24 hours before you plan to start sowing, place an ample number of seeds in a piece of lightweight cloth, tie it together, and soak the whole thing in a weak tea water solution. Then refrigerate the solution.

PLANTING UTENSILS

You'll need these items to start your seeds indoors:

Containers—try old pie or cake tins, cottage cheese cartons, plas tic butter tubs, or even styrofoam cups.

Tray—use any trays large enough to hold the containers.

Mister—any plastic spray bottle is suitable, but wash the bottle before you use it.

Long sharp pencil

Tweezers

Soil—use any of the professional planter mixes on the market, but not potting soil—it's too heavy.

Soil heat regulator—try a heating pad or warm surface on which to place the containers. The soil must remain at 68° to 72°F for seeds to sprout.

Full spectrum light —a 60-watt gro light will do.

PLANT WITH CARE

The care you take in handling your seeds will determine the quality of seedlings you produce. Plan ahead so you'll have plenty of time to plant carefully.

1. Wash each container with a mild solution of soap and ammonia before planting.

2. Fill each container with professional planter mix after you've added **2 tbsp. Epsom salts** per quart of mix. Dampen the mix (but don't soak it), level it off by gently tamping it down.

3. Use the pencil to make holes in the planter mix 1/4" deep, 2" apart.

4. Remove your seeds from the refrigerator. Spread them on a paper towel to dry so that you can pick them up with tweezers. Insert 1 seed in each hole (the effort is worth it).

5. Using your thumb, cover each seed with planter mix and press down lightly.

6. Put a weak tea solution into your mist bottle, adding **2 drops liquid dish soap, 2 drops ammonia and 1 drop whiskey.** Shake gently, then mist the surface of the newly planted seed containers.

7. Place the containers on a tray and cover with a towel that has been dampened with the tea solution. Place the tray in a dark, warm location for the next 4 days. If your house is cool, use a heating pad underneath the tray. Each day, raise the towel cover, mist lightly, dampen the towel, and cover the tray again.

8. On the sixth day, place the tray in a southern or eastern window with the 60 watt gro light on from 3 p.m. to 11 p.m. When 2 leaves sprout from each seed, it's time to move them.

9. To transplant your new seedlings, use a small spoon and remove as much of the planter mix as possible. Set the plants into individual 2-1/4" clay pots filled with fresh professional mix.

10. Feed the young plants with **liquid fish fertilizer (at 5% of the recommended rate), 2 drops liquid dish soap and 1 drop whiskey per quart of water.**

11. Treat the new seedlings like your other house plants until it's time to move them to the garden.

Nearly all flowers and bulbs can be started indoors. You can transplant many varieties into larger containers and keep them indoors or on your patio if you don't have garden space. In either case, they'll produce flowers that are worth every moment of the extra effort.

America's / Master Gardener®

SOIL
Testing & Repair

S oil testing sounds like a homework assignment from your high school biology instructor: complicated, time consuming, and confusing. It sounds worse than it actually is.

Soil testing is a simple chore that even a child can do. As a matter of fact, it's a great introduction to gardening for the future homeowner.

Testing your soil for acidity helps you decide how good a location is for a garden, lawn, or nursery stock. It also tells you when an old location has gone sour or developed a sweet tooth (alkaline). We call this the pH factor, and the scale runs from 0 to 14. 7.0 is neutral, with anything below considered to be acidic, and anything above, alkaline. As a rule, you will find that most lawn and garden soil runs from 6.0 to 7.5.

HOW TO TEST SOIL
Almost every garden center has a soil test kit on their shelves, from a $1.00 pH throw-away kit to the full soil test kits that cost several dollars. You can also buy mechanical meters that push into the ground to give you immediate pH, nitrogen, and many other readings. Or, you can call your local extension service, and they will give you an address where you can send your soil for testing.

HOW TO CORRECT SOIL CONDITIONS
As your interest in your garden increases, your understanding of the needs of the plants you befriend will improve. Like you, your plants can get upset stomachs, headaches, or hangovers from time to time, and they will look to you for relief. I suggest that each spring, you test the soil in all growing areas for the pH level, and make the necessary corrections before trouble rears its ugly head.

- **Correcting alkaline soil:** alkaline soil, known as sweet soil, can be corrected by adding a handful of sulphur per mature shrub, 1 tsp. per mature annual, perennial, or bulb plant, and 2 lbs. of ammonium sulphate per 100 square feet of garden. Leaves from an oak tree shredded with a power mower or leaf shredder are an excellent source of these nutrients.

- **Correcting acidic soil:** acidic soil is a simple condition to change. Adding 5 lbs. of limestone per 100 sq. ft. of area will do nicely. The following is the rule of thumb for applying lime per 1,000 sq. ft.

30 lbs. for sandy soil

50 lbs. for sandy loam

70 lbs. for loam

80 lbs. for clay soil

Never apply lime to a garden or lawn within 2 weeks of applying lawn fertilizer.

Flower growing success or failure can always be traced back to the quality of your soil. If most of the seeds, bulbs, or rooted cuttings you invite to grow around your home had a choice, they would hurt your feelings by declining your invitation. Why? Simply because most of the soil in both the flower and vegetable gardens in this country is weak in organic matter, and as a rule, there is little air space or water holding capacity in it.

While adding organic materials and combining soil types (such as sand, clay, and loam) are a form of preparation, there is a lot more to basic soil preparation. If you are to have an abundant, worry-free flower garden year after year, you must constantly improve the soil.

SOIL
Preparation

This chapter on flower growing starts with soil support for seeds, seedlings and bulbs. In the beginning of this booklet, I mentioned flower gardens, patio containers, and hanging baskets. This is what I mean by types of gardens, and along with this, you can add soil-less flower and bulb growing. I also want you to remember that raised flower gardens are as popular as vegetable gardens for many of the same reasons: quicker results and easier maintenance.

The different types of gardens and soil preparation for each are:

CONTAINER SOIL PREPARATION

The perfect blend of soil for all container grown garden plants is:

> 1/3 sharp sand
> 1/3 clay loam
> 1/3 organic matter or
> 1/3 professional mix

In addition to the soil mixture, I would like you to add per peck of soil:

> 1/2 cup Epsom salts
> 1/4 cup coffee grounds
> (rinse them clean)
> 4 egg shells (dried and
> crushed to powder)

RAISED BEDS

For each 50 sq. ft. of garden area, use the soil mix described in the container form and add:

> 10 lbs. lime
> 2-1/2 lbs. garden food
> 1/2 lb. Epsom salts

IN-GROUND SOIL PREPARATIONS

For each 50 sq. ft. of garden area, add:

> 15 lbs. pelletized lime
> 15 lbs. pelletized gypsum
> 5 lbs. garden food
> 1 lb. Epsom salts

Now you may spade and till in, or till in if your spading is done.

SELECTION

?

There should be a lot more to selecting flowers than simply looking at the pretty pictures in the mail order catalogs. But in most cases, that's how it begins and ends. That's unfortunate because there's a whole lot more.

Color, texture, form, and shape are the yardsticks of the professional gardener, followed by blooming time, and length of blooming time when it comes to planning and selecting flowers.

I have seen many home flower gardens and patio plantings that had all the right colors, heights, and bloom times, but because of the variety of foliage, looked like a planned mess. For cut flower gardens, you don't have to worry about anything but color, quality, and quantity, unless it's in the front yard. But when it comes to border and show plantings, you should best have your flower act together.

ANNUALS

Every home should have a cut-flower garden. I am not talking about the petunias or marigolds around the walkways, driveways and buildings, or a geranium or 2 in a tub on the patio. No, the hanging basket of impatiens doesn't quite qualify. Both of my Grandmothers, Putnam and Baker, had flower beds in every empty space you could find. Oh sure, there were border flowers, and the geraniums had their special places, but it was the cut flowers that were used to decorate the tables, bedrooms and as gifts for friends under the weather. That's what I want all of you folks to consider—cut-flower gardens.

America's / Master Gardener®

❓ ANNUALS

START FROM SCRATCH

It is tempting to buy already grown bedding plants, and I suggest that you do so for your border plantings. For the cut flower garden, however, let's use seeds. You may have to wait a little longer, but come July and August and even into September, it'll be worth the wait.

PLENTY TO PICK FROM

Of course, you will excuse my pun. Here are a few for you to consider:

Asters	Daisy, Tahoka	Nasturtium
Annual Dahlia	Gaillardia	Salpiglossis
Bachelor Buttons	Gerbera	Salvia
Bells of Ireland	Gomphrena	Scabiosa
Carnations	Larkspur	Snapdragon
Celossia	Marigold—	Verbena
Cosmos	medium & tall	Zinnia

IF YOU DON'T NEED A PICK, THEY WILL GROW!

It's not true that if you can get a crack into clay, Salvia will find a way. But as a rule, try to give your cut flowers at least 8" to 11" of medium soil to get a good footing. One of the best layouts I have seen in a long time is a series of 24" round circles dug from various locations in a lawn area, the depth of a long-handled spade with a 10" cut. These circles were filled with 1/2 ordinary soil, 1/2 professional planter mix, and then planted with different varieties.

GIVE IT SOME ARTISTIC CONSIDERATION!

You want to be able to enjoy the flowers while they grow, as well as enjoy them in bouquets, so try to keep height, color and texture in mind as you plant the seeds.

FLOWERS ARE GIRLS, SO WATCH THEIR DIETS!

If a plant has fruits, flowers, or vegetables, it's a girl and it's diet must contain a great deal of phosphorus and potash, and only a minimal amount of nitrogen. I've found that using a water soluble plant food mixed at half the recommended rate with 1/2 oz. liquid dish soap per gallon of water once every 2 weeks does the trick. In May and mid-July, I sprinkle Epsom salts onto the flower beds at a rate of 1/4 cup per 2' circle. Remember, feed before noon.

MY FLOWER BEDS NEVER WILT

The worst thing you can do to a flower is to let her spend herself and wilt on the stem. Flowers are born to bloom and bring beauty. Cut them early in the morning and place them in a vase that has **1 tbsp. of clear corn syrup and a pinch of Clorox® bleach** added to it. This will keep them center stage for days and sometimes even a week or 2 longer.

So you don't waste time, effort, and money shopping around, here is a list of annuals and their uses for quick reference:

Borders	Ageratum • Alyssum • Balsam • Bells of Ireland Centaurea • Cleome • Cosmos • Cynoglossum Larkspur • Marigold • Nicotiana • Petunia Salvia • Snapdragon • Statice • Zinnia
Color	Amaranthus • Basil • Canna • Coleus • Dusty Miller • Kochia • Perilla
Partial Shade	Balsam • Begonia • Browallia • Calendula • Coleus Impatiens • Lobelia • Myosotis • Nicotiana • Pansy Salvia • Torenia
Seaside	Alyssum • Dusty Miller • Hollyhock • Lupine Petunia • Statice
Window Boxes	Alyssum • Begonia semperflorens • Coleus • Cascade Petunias • Lobelia • Nierembergia • Thunbergia

America's / Master Gardener®

❓ ANNUALS

Edging   Ageratum • Alyssum • Begonias • Calendula
Candytuft • Dwarf Bachelor Buttons • Celosia
Coleus • Dianthus • Dusty Miller • Ganzania
Gomphrena • Heliotrope • Impatiens • Lobelia
Mesembryanthemum • Nierembegia • Phlox
Pansy • Petunia • Portulaca • Snapdragon
Torenia • Verbena • Vinca • Zinnia-dwarf

Cutting   Asters • Bachelor Buttons • Bells of Ireland • Carnation
Celosia • Cosmos • Cynoglossum • Dahlia
Daisy, Tahoka • Gaillardia • Gerbera • Gomphrena
Larkspur • Marigold • Nasturtium • Petunias
Rudbeckia • Salpiglossis • Salvia • Scabiosa
Snapdragons • Statice • Verbena • Zinnia

Medium   Balsam • Basil • Bells of Ireland • Carnation
Growers   Celosia (medium cristat types such as Fireglow)
(12" - 24")   Cynoglossum • Dahlia (such as Unwin's dwarf mix)
Dusty Miller • Gaillardia • Gomphrena •
Helichrysum • Impatiens • Nicotiana • Petunias
Rudbeckia • Salpiglossis • Salvia • Snapdragons

Tall   Amaranthus • Asters • Celosia • Bachelor Buttons
Growers   Cleome • Cosmos • Dahlia • Hollyhock • Larkspur
(3' - 5')   Marigolds • Scabiosa • Snapdragons • Statice
Zinnia

Ground   Cobaea • Creeping Zinnia • Lobelia
Covers   Mesembryanthemum • Morning Glory • Myosotis
Nasturtium • Nierembergia • Portulaca • Sweet
Alyssum • Sweet Pea • Thunbergia • Verbena
Vinca

Rock   Alyssum • Candytuft • Dusty Miller • Ganzania
Gardens   Ground covers • Mesembryanthemum • Pansy
Verbena

PERENNIALS

I f you've been investing too much green in flowers every spring, it's time you picked perennials. Flowering perennials are a practical, economical alternative to annuals. For just pennies, they'll add blooming bouquets for years to come.

You can grow dozens of varieties from seeds, tubers, or bulbs. All they need from you is a little watering, feeding and pest control help.

Perennials come in all sizes, shapes, heights, and colors: achilles, monarda, foxglove, begonia, iris, goldenrod, poppy, sedum, peony, gaillardia, and hibiscus. They're great for borders, dividers, decorating, covering problems—and they grow in all soils.

GOING TO SEED

If you're a beginner, select the perfect perennials for your gardening needs by leafing through mail-order seed catalogs. Any spring or fall catalog is bulging with pictures, growing information, and prices of perennial plants and seeds.

Many companies produce these catalogs, most of which are free. If your name isn't on a mailing list, send away for just one seed catalog. Your name will go through the catalog field faster than a bee with a bumble full of pollen headed for the hive! Soon you'll have a whole swarm of catalogs to look through.

Here's a list of several companies that offer catalogs with good perennial selections:

- **K. Van Bourgondien,** 245 Farmingdale Rd., Babylon, NY 11702
- **Park Seed Co.,** PO Box 46, Greenwood, SC 29648-0046
- **Thompson and Morgan,** Box 1308, Jackson, NJ 08527
- **W. Atlee Burpee Co.,** 300 Park Avenue, Warminister, PA 18974

To complement perennial selections and uncomplicate the annual color spend-a-thon, plant spring flowering bulbs as well as summer bulbs, and then sprinkle annual seeds—not plants—in designated spots each spring. Before you know it, you'll be enjoying expensive flowering plant colors at a fraction of the price of annuals.

Jerry Baker
America's / Master Gardener®

? PERENNIALS

TIPS TO GET YOU STARTED

Make sure you have a rich organic soil mix—perennials prefer it. Combine heavy soil with sand, perlite, sawdust, aged manure, grass, and leaves.

Feed perennials with a rose and flower systemic plant food in early spring. Every 3 weeks, give them a helping of liquid plant food—at half the recommended rate—mixed with **half a can of beer** to 10 gallons of water (use your 10 gallon hose-end sprayer.)

Then after 6:00 p.m., spray your perennials with this tonic in your 20 gal. hose-end sprayer, filling the balance of the jar with warm water:

1 cup liquid dish soap

6 tsp. Rose and Flower Dust

(made into a paste)

Always add a golf ball to your hose-end sprayer to agitate the mixture.

Hostas

Professional gardeners consider hostas to be the most important foliage perennials. These handsome plants, also known as shady lilies, grow in neat mounds with large, heart-shaped leaves. They make great ground cover, they do well in shady or sunny areas, live long, cost little, and require minimal care. They also come in a wide variety of foliage, colors, and textures. Some of the more popular varieties include Blue Umbrellas, Shade Fanfare, Antioch, Piedmont Gold, Montan Kabitan, Aureo-Marginata, Sum & Substance, Francee, and Aurora Boreobs.

Your local garden center should offer a good selection of hostas. If not, send for a free catalog from Wayside Gardens, P.O. Box 1, Hodges, SC 29695.

Wildflowers

Wildflowers are another perennial group that adds summer color to your corner of the world. Sow seeds in early spring. In many cases, the blooms will return year after year.

If you decide on wildflowers, remember that they tend to multiply and could end up taking over your yard. So plan well!

Different combinations of wildflower seeds are available for specific areas of the country. The best assortment for growing in all regions is: Black-Eyed Susans, Prairie Asters, Coreopsis, Chinese Houses, Purple Coneflowers, Indian Blankets and Tidy Lips.

Daylilies

Daylilies are popular perennials that require very little in the way of special attention. These blooming beauties, which are great for borders, feature attractive, lily-shaped flowers that can measure 6" in width. Some of the more popular varieties are Mary Todd, Sparkling Stars, Screech Owl, Sirocco, and Thousand Voices.

Plant daylilies in spring. First, dig a large hole in any type of soil and fill it with a mixture of leaves, grass clippings, sawdust, potting soil, and any other rich garden debris. Then pour this tonic into the planting hole.

1/2 can beer
1 oz. liquid dish soap
1 oz. ammonia
1 oz. fish fertilizer
1/2 oz. hydrogen peroxide
1/4 tsp. instant tea
in 2 gal. warm water

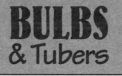

BULBS
& Tubers

Selecting bulbs and tubers can be a real chore, especially when it comes to planting fall bulbs for late winter to early summer color in your garden. More than once, the local squirrels have sat on a limb high in a tree or on a nearby fence, and chattered away at me for digging too close to a recently hidden nut. Just the opposite is true when I catch a mischievous off-spring of one of my long-time fancy-tailed friends high-balling it across the yard with one of my newly planted crocus bulbs in his teeth.

America's Master Gardener®

❓ BULBS

In the west and south, you have absolutely no excuse other than you are too lazy to plant. When bulbs are offered for sale at your favorite garden center, go to it. In the colder climates, you should wait until after the first frost, and then begin your project. In the north, crocus, daffodils, snow drops and scilla can be planted directly into an appropriate area of the lawn itself. In most cases, pushing a spade down and forward, dropping in a bulb, and then lifting out the spade and stepping on the spot does the job.

In the garden, dig a trench the proper depth, width, and length. Pile soil along both sides. Simply set the bulbs on the bottom, spaced at the proper distance. Sprinkle liberally with this mixture:

1/3 cup Epsom salts

2/3 cup bone meal

1/2 cup paradichlorobenzene

crystals mix per peck of soil

Then re-cover the bulbs and your job is done. If you prefer a bulb planter, pre-dig the holes, placing the soil cores in a basket, bucket, or wheelbarrow tray and breaking them up with a shovel. Then mix in the above mixture and use this to recover the bulbs.

You have to know when to plant. In the northern border states, September and early October, after a heavy frost, are best. In southern Michigan, Illinois, Missouri, Kansas and across the land to Colorado, October and November are good. In the south and west, it's December and January.

Just how long you can expect bulbs to bloom will really surprise you, as the chart on the next page indicates. Also, consult the mail order catalogs before planting.

If varmints (squirrels, raccoons, skunks, gophers, and shrews) are a problem, then lightly spray the bulbs with a material called Bone Tar Oil. It also takes care of deer and beaver.

Bulb	March	April	May	June
Snowdrops	■			
Winter Aconite	■			
Crocus	■			
Glory of Snow	■			
Early Tulips	■			
Red Emperor Tulips		■	■	
Grape Hyacinths		■		
Trumpet Daffodil		■		
Tulips Double Early		■		
Breeder Tulips			■	
Scilla			■	
Lily-flowered Tulips			■	■
Double Late Tulips			■	■
Double Late Tulips			■	■
Darwin Tulips			■	■
Parrot Tulips			■	■
Cottage Tulips			■	■
Dutch Iris			■	■

BULB TYPES

This group of flowers are grown from tubers, tuberous roots, and rhizomes. Unlike true bulbs and corms, these do not produce offspring from themselves, but neither does the potato, the most famous tuber. Gloxinias, caladium and gloriosa lilies are increased by cutting them into pieces with 1 eye to each piece, like you would a potato. Dahlias, on the other hand, need a little more tender handling when you divide them.

STARTING SEEDS
Outdoors

This section deals with growing annual flowers from seeds planted directly into the soil, right where you want them to grow.

It doesn't matter whether you are planting seeds or seedlings. The soil must be prepared the same way, and the results you get depend upon the quality of that preparation.

To begin, always add this prep mix per 100 sq. ft. of soil. Spade, till, and rake the area. Then add the liquid elements to your 10 gal. hose-end sprayer and over-spray with this tonic.

Prep Mix

2 bags peat moss

50 lbs. gypsum

2 lbs. Epsom salts

Liquid Elements:

1/2 can beer

1/2 cup liquid dish soap

4 oz. Vitamin B-1

Planting is easy. Place fine seeds on the surface of the soil, making sure that you don't have thick or thin patches of seed. Next, cover the seeds with a very thin layer of soil. No annual should be planted deeper than 1/4". Remember that it's better to plant too shallow, than too deep. Firm the soil with a light pat of your hand, foot, hoe or flat board.

After planting your seeds, water lightly and cover with a single sheet of newspaper for 2 days, dampen the paper and remove it 2 days later.

SPACING SEEDS

Spacing seeds (like seedlings) to give them room to grow takes a little more time, but it also saves you the time and trouble of thinning and transplanting later. I take the time to poke a small hole or space in a seed trench, cover each seed, water, and walk away content with the thought that each seed has had my personal attention. It does make a difference!

SPEEDING UP SPROUTING

The sooner my seeds can pop their heads above ground, the better chance they have to compete with weeds before you can mulch them with newspaper, plastic or grass clippings.

SEEDS & SEEDLINGS CAN SHARE THE SAME BED

The main purpose behind a flower garden is to have flowers for both indoor and outdoor decoration, from 1 end of the growing season to the other. One way to do that is to interplant seeds with seedlings. I put in my early seeds, place a marker next to them, and leave enough room between for seedlings to be planted. 2 weeks later, I plant the seedlings. I make a shallow hole (1/4") between the new seed sprouts and the seedlings, and plant other seeds of the same variety. This is called "delayed progressive planting", and results in fresh, full, colorful, compact plants from spring through fall.

SEEDLINGS

Remember what I said about getting the soil ready? It doesn't matter whether you're planting seeds or seedlings, you've got to prepare the soil the same way.

A seedling is a plant grown from seed indoors, under lights, by you or a professional grower. When it comes to selecting and planting annual seedlings, make sure you pick the healthiest, strongest looking plants. With a relatively short growing season, you can't waste a lot of time and space.

The 5 most popular and widely used annuals are: zinnias, marigolds, salvia, impatiens, and petunias. Each of these varieties comes in several different colors and heights, so be sure to read the tag or package so you don't hide the short ones in the rear.

PURCHASING ANNUAL PLANTS

The secrets to buying the best plants are simple:

1. Try to purchase your annuals between 10 a.m. and 11 a.m. because the garden center operator has probably just returned from the early produce market with fresh plants or his grower has just delivered fresh flats.

2. Whenever possible, try to select your flower packs from inside flats, since they have less damage from the truck ride.

3. Purchase very short plants with little or no color showing.

4. Never purchase tall, lanky, full-flowered annuals because you will first have to cut them back.

5. Plant your annuals the day you bring them home.

A week after putting in your new plants, pinch out the center to stimulate low branching. Sprinkle Epsom salts on the soil. Then cover the soil with newspaper and grass clippings if you are not going to interplant with seeds.

MULCH

Very few home gardeners ever think of mulching the soil around flowers. They think of mulch only as a decorative covering of stone and wood chips around trees, shrubs, and evergreens. Even then, they don't really know why they use a mulch, other than it looks good.

Well, mulch simulates the plants' natural growing conditions. Proper use of a good mulch can mean the difference between super, healthy-looking plants, with prolonged bloom time, and struggling, puny, unhealthy-looking foliage and flowers.

TYPES OF MULCH

ORGANIC:
Grass clippings, straw, buckwheat shells, leaves, compost, rotted manure, corn cob particles, coco bean shells, and shredded newspaper.

INORGANIC:
Plastic sheeting, plastic fabric, shingles, and roofing paper.

Why bother mulching? There are lots of reasons, but the most common are:
- Prevent soil scorch surface tension
- Maintain even soil moisture and temperature
- Prevent evaporation
- Organic soil builder
- Insect and disease trap
- Prevent weeds
- Eliminate cultivating

▣ MULCH

If at all possible, use organic mulch. They're better for your plants and the environment. To mulch, place a single sheet of newspaper on the soil beneath flowers, and lightly dust the paper with swimming pool filter dust (diatomaceous earth) and 1/2 pound of Epsom salts per 50 sq. ft. of garden. Then cover the newspaper with 4" to 6" of grass clippings, or 3" of other organic mulch. Do not use peat moss. The swimming pool earth discourages insects, so mix it into the mulch as you pile the mulch on.

The inorganic mulches—plastic, shingles, and roofing paper, are best used under decorative stone around trees, shrubs, and evergreens, except in the dry, hot parts of the country. In those areas, I would only use the new plastic cloth (black or white), or roofing paper.

Mulch is a must if you want a beautiful, worry-free and work-free flower garden. Also, in fall, mulch protects roots and bulbs from the thaw-freeze syndrome that causes winter heaving.

FEEDING

F eeding is the most misunderstood, confusing and scary job, and it shouldn't be. When it comes to fertilizers, you either use too much, not enough, or, in defense and despair, none at all.

My friends, the 3 numbers on a fertilizer bag are not the odds on your plants living or dying when you use it, unless you use it wrong. They simply tell you the percentage of nutrients - nitrogen, phosphate and potash - that are in the fertilizer.

KINDS OF PLANT FERTILIZER

ORGANIC FERTILIZERS are the manure types made from animal waste, decayed plants, animals or fish such as liquid seaweed, liquid fish fertilizer, or dried blood, all of which are slower acting and safer.

INORGANIC FERTILIZERS are chemical mixtures and compounds that are more concentrated fertilizers which can easily burn if not properly used.

It is best to use a combination of both, along with proper timing. In fall, your garden should have 4 pounds of any dry garden food sprinkled on top of the soil and turned under. Do the same with manure, leaving it to rest in the soil all winter. In spring, you should top dress (spread on top of the soil) your garden with 1/2 pound of Epsom salts and 5 pounds of bone meal before tilling.

Flowers should not fed for their first 3 weeks in the ground. Thereafter, begin a regular feeding program (every 3 weeks) by alternating these 2 tonics every time you feed.

NUMBER 1	NUMBER 2
15-30-15 liquid fertilizer	1 oz. liquid fish fertilizer
at half the recommended rate	1 oz. bourbon
1 cup beer	2 tbsp. instant tea
1/4 cup liquid dish soap	in 2 gal. warm water
in 1 gal. warm water	

WATERING

Let your flowers tell you when they need water, and then soak them from the soil level. Don't water again until the foliage appears to be thirsty, which means that it is slightly wilting.

Initially, place a hose into a bucket and let it fill and run over into trenches you have cut between rows, before you cover the soil with newspaper and mulch. You can soak the soil with a hose flaring nozzle, soaker hose, or a wicket set a little higher than your garden.

Seldom, if ever, water your flowers from the top because you can damage them very easily. If you are properly mulching the soil, the time of day seldom makes a difference when you water.

WEED
Controls

 W eeds can be stopped or controlled by:

- Using a good, heavy mulch like we discussed earlier.

- Applying products that I like to call the "kneeless weeders". They are pre-emergent weed controls which means they won't let weeds germinate as long as they are not disturbed when they are applied to the soil. Try them, you'll like what they do for you and your garden

- The old fashioned, "armstrong" way - by being pulled up, dug up or cut off. This, however, never seems to result in permanent control.

- Applying any of the systemic weed killers like Systemic Grass and Weed Killer, Kleenup®, Round-Up®, or Shoot Out®. **These products kill whatever they touch from the top down,** including your annuals, perennials or bulb stock if they touch the foliage. So be very careful when applying any of these controls. But if you have a weed that just won't go away, you can paint it's foliage and avoid other plants with great success.

INSECT &
Disease Controls

here is no way to keep all insects away from your yarden. But to discourage insects and prevent disease, bathe your flowers every 2 weeks, in the evening, with this tonic applied with your 20 gal. hose-end sprayer.

1/2 cup liquid dish soap
1/2 cup antiseptic mouthwash
1/2 cup chewing tobacco juice*
fill the balance of the sprayer jar
with warm water.

At the first sign of trouble, mix this tonic in a gallon of water and apply with a 20 gal. hose-end sprayer. Place a golf ball in the sprayer jar to agitate the tonic.

6 tsp. Tomato/Vegetable Dust
(made into a paste)
1 tbsp. liquid dish soap
fill the balance of the sprayer jar
with warm water.

THE HIT LIST

There are somewhere between 18 and 24 common insects that can disturb your flower garden. Here's a list of the usual suspects:

INSECTS

Aphid, Army Worm, Bulb Mites, Flea Beetle, Iris Borer, Japanese Beetles, Leaf Miners, Saw Bug, Striped Cucumber Beetle, Spider Mites, Thrips, Gladiolus Thrips, Snails, Narcissus Bulb Fly Larvae, Slugs, Nematodes, Grasshopper, Wire Worms

CHEMICAL CONTROLS

The chemical controls to combat these pests include:

Malathion, Pyrethrum, Soap, Dursban, Diazinon, Sevin, Methoxychlor, Metaldehyde, Rotenone, Nicotine, Bacillus Thuringiensis, Bacillus Poppillae, Paradichlorobenzene, Captan, Zineb, Phalthar, baby powder (bulbs, corms, tubers)

Start with the least powerful control, and if that fails, try something stronger. And remember, only use chemical controls for their recommended uses at their recommended rates!

*To make chewing tobacco juice, place 3 fingers of chewing tobacco in an old nylon stocking and soak it in a gallon of hot water until the mixture is dark brown.

NOTES

America's Master Gardener®